SIDÓNIO PAIS AND THE NEW REPUBLIC

December 1917-December 1918

SIDÓNIO PAIS AND THE NEW REPUBLIC

December 1917-December 1918

Jamie Stewart Jones

Sidónio Pais and the New Republic:
December 1917-December 1918
Jamie Stewart Jones

CPHRC Editorial Services
506-508 Strathmartine Road
Dundee DD39BR
Scotland
cphrc@cphrc.co.uk

Thank you

Thank you so much for purchasing our book! Your support is truly appreciated. We hope that you find the content valuable and engaging.

As you dive into the pages, we would be incredibly grateful if you could take a moment to leave an honest review on Amazon. Your feedback is essential to us and helps others make informed decisions about their reading choices.

Honest reviews, whether positive or constructive, play a crucial role in supporting our small business and enabling us to improve.

Thank you once again for your purchase and for being part of our journey. We look forward to hearing your thoughts and hope you enjoy the book!

To leave a review, please follow these steps:

1. Go to Amazon and search for the product name or ASIN.
2. Navigate to the product page.
3. Scroll down to the reviews section.
4. Click on "Write a customer review" to leave your feedback.

A brief note

This essay was written about 25 years ago, was presented at a seminar and then found its way into a box that was gradually forgotten over the years.

I recently decided to have a clear out of old boxes that were cluttering up a space I suddenly decided I needed. That is when I rediscovered a large collection of papers that I had written back when I was researching and writing about the Portuguese First Republic. This is one of these papers, which I think deserves to see the light of day again.

Unfortunately, however, I cannot find the pages on which the references were written—perhaps I didn't print them out! I really can't remember. So, for that I apologise. I have included the ones that I managed to track down.

Jamie Stewart Jones
Dundee, October 2024

Sidónio Pais and the New Republic

While much stress has been placed on the military nature of the Sidónio Pais coup of 5 December 1917, this itself has become a form of shorthand for the nature of and reasons for the military's endorsement.

It is clear Sidónio did, in fact, have widespread support within the armed forces, but it is equally clear that the armed forces themselves were divided, and that they were driven by a whole range of concerns and ideals.

But this fact has been recognised by historians is clear in the different motivations they attribute to the military as an institution.

For example, Ribeiro de Meneses (1998a) implies that elements within the armed forces, particularly

Democratic Party officers serving in the Portuguese Expeditionary Corps (CEP), were reacting against Afonso Costa's refusal to launch a public inquiry into the alleged atrocities committed by General Pereira d'Eça in Africa.

Medeiros Ferreira (1992: 69-72) says the Sidonista coup was the result of a fracture within the armed forces between those who sought to reduce the size of the CEP at all costs, thereby reducing Portugal's involvement in the European war, and those who believed that Portugal should prosecute the war to the full extent of its abilities.

Despite, or perhaps because of this inability to discover any single motive for the military's involvement, many historians have argued that its response (and its divisions) was merely symptomatic of wider divisions within Portuguese society on the eve of Sidónio's uprising.

While the armed forces remain an important factor in the success of the 1917 coup, it is not regarded as the only, or even as the most important actor in this process.

Rather, there seems to be a general consensus that Sidónio (and Sidonismo) was the beneficiary of several disparate factors, at least initially, and thought this fact is quite clearly reflected in the weight range of disparate groupings that rallied to his side during the days and weeks following the overthrow of the liberal Republic.

Telo (1998) demonstrates the devastating effects the war had on Portuguese society, and which drastically altered the relationship between the rulers and the ruled.

Among the items he lists as being most significant (1998: 14) are: the reduction of imports to one-third of their normal level; the advent of inflation; famine; and increased state intervention in the economy, combined with a situation of military defeats and an altered strategic situation that made Portuguese involvement in the war seem both unnecessary and undesirable, both from the point of view of the Allied and Portuguese high commands and of the Portuguese people.

Ribeiro de Meneses (1998b: 11) develops this last point further when he argues that anti-war feeling was widespread in Portugal, with Afonso Costa's open-ended commitment to the war effort through—the supply of 4000 fresh troops each month particularly resented.

Medeiros Ferreira points out (1992: 70) that many, especially (although not exclusively) within the army, saw in the entry of the United States into the war and the necessarily altered logistical situation to be an honourable way out for a poorly supplied corps that believed itself to be a little more than political cannon fodder for the Democratic Party.[1]

Anti-war feeling in Portugal was, however, itself

both the cause and the result of several factors, not all of which were directly related to Portugal's physical involvement as a belligerent.

One of the main causes of wartime discontent in metropolitan Portugal was the subsistence crisis that became particularly acute during the summer and autumn of 1917.

Medeiros (1978: 111-43) argued that this crisis was itself the result of 'currency depreciation, commercial and financial deficits... and an "ever more aggressive" proletariat'.

In his analysis of wartime Portugal, he clearly states these were factors that were largely independent of Portugal's involvement in the war—although he does acknowledge that they were exacerbated by the '"war economy"... which demonstrated that the "agrarian economy" was the most sensitive economic sector when faced with political and military imperatives' (1978: 122).

Schwartzmann (1987: 145-58) adopts a similar position in her assertion that Portugal's economy during the First Republic was essentially dualist and disarticulated, with the result that neither the industrial nor the agrarian elites, both of which were represented within the political regime, could reach any form of agreement between themselves.

She develops this idea further in her monologue (1989) in which she states her belief that the urban bourgeoisie's rise to political dominance after 1913 led to a breakdown in the 'vertical and horizontal political parts' that had hitherto ensured the continuing hegemony of the Democratic Party as it became increasingly clear that the interests of the separate groups were essentially incompatible rather than merely conflicting.[2]

A further spin on the concept of a rural/urban conflict is developed by Costa Pinto (1982; 1992; 1994) and Braga da Cruz (1980; 1982; 1986) in their analysis of the development of the traditionalist ideologies that were being promoted by a wide range of political movements, from the monarchists to the Catholics, during the period up to and beyond 1917.

Their analyses, while reaching similar conclusions to those presented by Schwartzmann, differ insofar as they seem to argue the economic dualism that existed was the result of much deeper-rooted social divisions typical of societies in the process of social modernisation and development.

For the two Portuguese historians, the prevailing problem in Portugal was that an inherently conservative rural sector was desperately attempting to preserve a way of life that was being undermined by the growth of large urban areas.

Conversely, historians like Schwartzmann seem to argue that the maintenance of traditionalist ruralist ideals, and the transfer of these ideals to the urban milieu, was creating 'tension between the actual state of economic activities in the country and the great promise inherent in such a development' (Gershenkron 1966: 114).

A notable fact, highlighted by Telo (1998: 15), is that Sidónio's coup took place in the capital and represented 'the first time the Democratic Party had been defeated in Lisbon'.

Explicit in this comment is the recognition that 'the streets are against it' and, implicitly, that the role of the urban working class was in some way significant in assisting in the success of the revolt.

This working-class contribution could be positive, in that the Lisbon proletariat were at best active in their support of the uprising or at worst passive onlookers.

Telo's other assertion that Sidónio was supported by elements ranging from the extreme nationalist right all the way through to the anarcho-syndicalist left is somewhat undermined by his later argument (1998: 19-20) that Sidonismo was a modernising phenomenon that had emerged as a direct response to the 'crisis of state authority in the Portuguese context'.

Furthermore, the fact that the revolution occurred in Lisbon lends credence to the belief the urban proletariat's contribution was essentially negative—that is to say, that to the extent there was urban bourgeois support for the uprising, this was the result of a growing fear of a militant and increasingly powerful workers' movement.

Medeiros (1978: 133-43) makes a powerful case when he argues that the power of the Lisbon industrial proletariat has been exaggerated by analysts who have, in the absence of alternative sources, taken statistics for Lisbon and applied them to the country as a whole without commenting on the fact that 'the region of Porto was, during the war, the country's principal industrial region (1978: 135).

Figures presented by Stanley Payne (1973: 575) and Medeiros (1978: 75) show that Portugal's industrial working class in 1917 numbered almost 130,000, 57,000 of whom were women and children (see Appendix).

While almost half of this proletariat was employed in the Lisbon area, Payne further shows that the average size of the Lisbon factory was one-third the size of its northern counterpart.[3]

It is quite clear that factories in the north were larger and employed more women and children to perform work that was largely unskilled, such as in the textile industry, which accounted for 28.3% of the working population and which was located in the area around Porto in the north and Tomar in the centre of the country, with an average factory size of 78 workers (Medeiros 1978: 75-89).

The textile industry was by far the largest industrial sector, at least in terms of employment.

The next largest was food processing, which employed 24,606 or 19.3% of the industrial working class in 1917. This important industry was concentrated in the Algarve, where 50 factories employed 7000 people, and in Setúbal where 63 factories employed 5000.

The remaining 53% of the working class was employed in the remaining 4009 factories, approximately 2500 of which were in Lisbon, with the remainder spread throughout the rest of the country (Medeiros 1978: 75-89; Payne 1973: 575).

Medeiros (1978: 74) goes even further in drawing conclusions from these statistics when he claims that 'the two-thirds of the total number of factories counted that employed fewer than ten people cannot be classed as industrial, even if they cannot truly be classed as artisanal'.

In this grey area between the truly proletarianised working class and the semi-skilled and unskilled working class lay the vast majority of Lisbon's working-class population, although Rosas (1994: 91-2) does point out that:

> The Lisbon region... contains the greatest concentration of 'pure' working class, in the sense that it is there that the processes of capitalist development have created an extended and radical separation of the waged industrial producers from the instruments of production... That is to say, it is the region in which the labour force lives primarily by sell-

> ing its labour, where class relationships are much more pronounced, where class conflict tends to be most exacerbated and where the propensity to take industrial and political action is most noticeable.

In the north, however, the form of industry, despite the larger unit size, was 'pre-capitalist': 'from São João de Madeira to the large cotton mills of Braga... the "industrial semi-proletariat" dominates.

An industrial labour force that is simultaneously peasant... supplementing their incomes' (Rosas 1994: 91).

Field (1951: 426) reminds us that in the wake of the Bolshevik Revolution, 'a deep and pervasive fear spread throughout strictly upper-class circles and filtered down in greater or lesser degree to all who had something to lose besides their chains'.

Medeiros (1978: 151) also refers to the climate of violent confrontation that had been engendered in Portugal as a result of the strike wave of the summer and autumn of 1917, to which Afonso Costa's government had initially responded by mobilising strikers and making them subject to martial law,[4] and when that failed to produce the desired effect—and moreover 'illuminated by the news of the October Revolution'—through the creation of civilian 'Republican Defence Groups' (Medeiros 1978: 150-1).

Given the absence of details outlining the membership of these groups, it is reasonable to assume they were physical manifestations of the fears of the urban petit-bourgeoisie, not only of an imminent working-class revolution but also of its concern that the government, given its inability throughout the autumn of 1917 to control the working classes, was on the brink of capitulation to the strikers.

For their own part, the organised working class had their reasons for seeking the overthrow of the Republican regime that had done very little to protect or advance their interests.

Afonso Costa's 'sympathy' for the class struggle in a speech of July 1917 (Oliveira Marques 1975: 30) was regarded as a rhetorical ploy by the workers who continued to see Costa and the party he led as being only 'apparently liberal', and judged him to be no better than José de Almeida's Evolutionist Party, whose 'conservative premise was sufficient to hinder popular progress', and Brito Camacho's Unionist Party of the 'Republican elite'.

As far as the workers were concerned, these parties were 'nothing more than the beginnings of a predominantly reactionary movement' (Sousa 1989: 24) whose real goal was to prevent any alteration of the prevailing social structure and to protect a pseudo-democratic system that guaranteed bourgeois political control (Schwartzman 1989: 178).

The organised working class saw little to celebrate

in the rise of the new regime, especially as it was also being supported by Brito Camacho and Egaz Moniz,[5] and merely adopted 'an attitude of benevolent neutrality' towards it (Robinson 1979: 37), thanks largely to Sidónio's promise to release the hundreds of workers who had been imprisoned by the previous government (Medeiros 1978: 152).

The Catholics' relationship with Sidónio's regime was not fully straightforward either (Braga da Cruz 1980: 270-4).

While the new regime courted Catholic favour by immediately reversing the previous government's decision to exile the bishops of Braga and of Évora and rescinding the orders preventing several priests from living in the parishes under their charge, the Church remained suspicious of Sidónio's nationalist project.

Preferring to remain independent of the regime, the religious authorities retained their own political organisation and continued their campaign against the regime's failure to end lay control of local parishes by its refusal to disband the lay committees that had been established by the Democrats in 1911.

The only conclusion that can reasonably be drawn from all the studies into the causes of and support for Sidónio's regime is that the legitimacy of its predecessor had been brought into question by a large and diverse section of Portuguese society.

The Democratic Party's hegemonic control of

the reins of political power was largely built upon the fact that it 'inherited the electoral machine of the liberal monarchy' (Costa Pinto 1998: 4), a process Farelo Lopes (1994: 41-50) has described as 'adherence'.[6]

Cabral (1979: 415) emphasises this continuity between the New Republic regime and the constitutional monarchy when he indicates that the Republic 'made use of the very same mechanisms of personalised pressure and the same electoral manipulations—in sum, those political mechanisms that were well known from the oligarchic *caciques*'.

Further arguments in this vein are advanced by Pulido Valente (1974) whose analysis of the role of the monarchist *caciques* on the advent of the New Republic leads him to the conclusion that these very political bosses merely sought to retain their political control by ensuring they had access to the Republican Party's commissions as well as to the local administrative bodies (Farelo Lopes 1994: 24-5).

One important consequence of the maintenance of the previous regime's 'clientelist' machinery was the rapid abandonment of the Republicans' previous policy in support of universal suffrage.

The electoral law of 14 March 1911 'postponed' the introduction of universal suffrage until some later and undefined date and although it did extend the franchise to 'heads of households' (Oliveira

Marques 1979:135),[7] it maintained the previous electoral law's literacy and tax clauses.[8] This, however, proved to be a temporary measure, as a new electoral law was introduced on 3 July 1913 that effectively restored the monarchist legislation of 1895 by removing heads of households, members of the armed forces and of the police, and women from the franchise. This new law resulted in a much smaller franchise than had existed at any time under the constitutional monarchy.

The fact the Republicans reversed their previous hostility to an electoral system that had been designed and implemented to frustrate them when an opposition, and instead restricted it even further once in power, was seen by some as a betrayal and by others as indicative of the desire of the new rulers to cling to power at any cost (Vasconcelos 1923).

Telo's argument (1998:15-16) would seem to cast some much-needed light on the debate regarding the Democratic Party's attitude towards the electorate.

He contends the franchise was restricted in both 1911 and 1913 as a result of the republican elite's recognition of the fact that in Portugal, as throughout southern Europe at the time, they had not been 'naturally and gradually replaced' as they had in the more developed countries of the north.

> Southern Europe had a different rhythm, with mass democracy only

> appearing after the Second World War in the case of Italy and during the 1970s in the cases of Spain, Portugal and Greece. At the beginning of the 20th century, Portugal was only weakly urbanised; it had a small urban middle class; it was weakly industrialised; there were no mass political parties; it had a politically independent elite; a protectionist economy; and the political power was regarded as the intermediary between the various corporate interests over access to privileges. The Republicans recognised this, hence the restricted franchise and maintenance of censorship. The Republic, therefore, was an elitist democracy not dissimilar to the constitutional monarchy, except in the fact that it was based in the urban rather than the rural milieu (Telo 1998: 15-16).

Robinson (1979: 36) is much less forgiving in his assessment of the Republicans' electoral policies, claiming that the restricted franchise was nothing less than a reflection of Afonso Costa's political prejudice against women, the urban working classes and the rural masses—all of whom were excluded from the electoral system by the 1913 law. Women were susceptible to clerical influence,[9] the urban working classes prey to demagogues and the rural masses to manipulation by the forces of reaction.

The ultimate failure of the Republicans to legitimate the Republic along lines that did not emulate the constitutional monarchy it had succeeded was, therefore, a direct consequence of its inability to meet the multifaceted challenges with which it was faced.

The heterogeneous nature of the Republic's initial support, which included sections of the army, particularly in Lisbon,[10] the Navy and an 'active urban minority' (Telo 1998: 12),[11] would seem to suggest that the desire to raise a new regime was essentially driven by negative motives: that is to say, it was much less a popular revolution than it was a rebellion against a governmental regime guilty of economic and political mismanagement.

Once in power, the Republican politicians, and Democratic Party politicians in particular, abandoned all attempts at ideological justification and instead acted to demobilise the popular elements that had been responsible for the events of October 1910 and began to adapt the existing institutions of the constitutional monarchy in such a way as to secure their position.[12]

Indeed, Schwarzmann (1989: 33-4) gives a very good illustration of this:

> Despite anarchist and socialist support for the revolution, the revolution was not against the Portuguese upper classes.

> After the rebellion, Neves observed banks, stores and houses of monarchist politicians being guarded by civilian elements of the revolution—including anarchists.[13]

This would seem to suggest that the Republic itself was little more than a tactical realignment, and that there was no real desire among leading Republicans for a more far-reaching revolutionary alteration in the form of government.

The nature of the regime was quite simply not an issue for most leading Republicans, a fact that eventually allowed monarchist forces, including the armed forces, to maintain an attitude of muted acceptance towards the Republic.

It can then be argued that the religious question, while undoubtedly an important part of the Republican ideology, was used as a diversion, for the Church could be seen to be an easy target that could distract the attention of the popular groups from the fact the new regime was not disposed to embark on a series of political and social reforms.

Yet this left the Republicans between a rock and a hard place. Their obvious reluctance to enact more than the most modest social reforms served only to alienate the support of the urban working classes, while what limited reforms they did introduce (for example, the right to strike and the reduction in the working week) were viewed with some hostility by important sectors of the urban middle classes.

Fhe Republicans' half-hearted attempts at land reforms, particularly through their abolition of the system of *enfiteuse,*[14] and their encouragement of the establishment of rural trade unions, also raised the spectre and the promise of revolutionary change without delivering it, thereby alienating what little goodwill existed towards the Republic in the rural areas.[15]

Perhaps the most significant factor in the disaggregation of the Republic was the unwillingness of the republican leaders to take concerted action against the disloyal opposition that existed within the armed forces (Linz 1978).

There was no purge of monarchist officers in the wake of the Republic's implantation, with the result that known monarchists, such as Pimenta de Castro and Gomes da Costa, were able to retain their positions (Medeiros Ferreira 1992: 43-4).

By failing to confront the army, the politicians of the Republic encouraged the development of disloyal elements and were responsible for the growth of military praetorianism and its subsequent ability and, importantly, its willingness to shape government policy either through direct intervention or by the mere threat of intervention.[16]

Contemporary observers of the new regime naturally found it very difficult to distinguish the several strands of thought that merged into its heterogeneous support base.

A commonly held view, and one that was promoted by the regime itself, was that Sidonismo was a conscious reaction against the failures of the liberal regime that it had overthrown.[17]

More than this, however, Sidónio represented the re-emergence of a national spirit and enthusiasm that had been buried by an elite that had, for almost a century, introduced false ideologies that promoted immediate interests to the detriment of the hopes of the entire people: 'Sidónio was the representative of those profound energies, those that became conscious in the enthusiasm of his name, those that included the form of action that had to be followed' (Castro 1924: 14-15).

It was an opinion that was advanced by the new regime's leaders in the very first public statement made by the Revolutionary Committee as they attempted to justify their actions:

> The Republic that was generously proclaimed on 5 October and then miserably betrayed by a political caste who audaciously conquered power and exploited it in their own interests to the serious injury of the nation, has triumphed. However, justice, the honest and impartial execution of the law, of order and of authority belongs to those who risk

> their lives for the nation and for the Republic.[18]

This was restated a few days later by Sidónio on taking office as Foreign Minister on 12 December 1917: 'Despite the Republic being only seven years old, it is possible to note the existence of corrupted customs that in all respects remind us of the long poisoning or Portuguese politics. The revolutionaries have made great efforts to regenerate these customs, to reintegrate the Republic in its purity, to strengthen the nation. It is a difficult task, but it is not impossible' (Pais 12 December 1917).

Yet this raises the question of Sidónio's own position.

Contemporary observers, much more so than modern investigators, have indicated that the heterogeneity of Sidónio's initial support was a source of strength rather than of weakness (Castro 1924; Raposo 1945; Vasconcelos 1923), insofar as it symbolised a widespread and multifaceted opposition to regime that had failed to live up to its initial promise, a regime that in the final analysis was less revolutionary than it was dictatorial: one that was, 'in contrast to the relative liberalism of political life in the "golden age" of the constitutional monarchy, closer to a de facto dictatorship... that marked the beginning of the end of the bourgeoisie's democratic institutions' (Pereira 1978: 9).

Sidónio's discourse always stressed the nature of his intervention as a means to end the 'rule of the demagogues', his shorthand for the Democratic Party in general and Afonso Costa in particular, and at no point does he question the legitimacy of the republican form—even when he was subjected to enormous pressure to change his position in the wake of Brito Camacho's decision on the eve of the parliamentary elections, in March 1918, to withdraw the Unionist Party's support for the New Republic—a fact pointed out by a leading integralist, Hipólito Raposo, in his discussion of Sidónio's rejection of the Integralist proposal for a new constitution:

> In truth, he only modified one article and substituted the monarch with the person of the president... After his return from a journey to the south of the country, which was followed by Brito Camacho's withdrawal of support because of the dismissal of Aresta Branco from the Council of Ministers, Sidónio's conduct displayed signs of fearful reservation. Of the constitution, read and studied by some of his ministers, nothing more was heard for the remainder of his consulate (Raposo 1945: 37).

A few weeks before these events, Sidónio had made

his position regarding monarchism and republicanism crystal clear:

> Both the extreme right and the extreme left seek to misinterpret the intentions of the movement of 5 December. Thus, we hear some saying that if we are to continue with the same regime, then there is no point in labouring, while others say that the revolution was pointless if we are to continue with the Republic. This is wrong; because the revolution was made to implant a new regime in which both monarchists and republicans can live. It was the party routine that was the evil (Pais 26 February 1918).

In an interview with the editor of the *Diário Nacional* during one of his visits to the north of the country, Sidónio restated his belief that his revolution was motivated by both the need and the popular demand for an end to the rule of the Democratic Party, rather than by any desire to overthrow the Republic: 'We have liberated the country from the oligarchy of the Democratic Party and have substituted it with a government of freedom and of morality' (Pais 11 February 1918).

This stance was re-emphasised at a speech in Santarém in which he claimed that: 'the revolution of 5 December defeated the men of the political parties' (Pais 4 March 1918), and yet again in his speech following his election as President in May 1918:

> All of the acts of the government of the Republic since the revolution of 5 December have been inspired by the purest republican faith and have been designed to ensure the consolidation of the Republic through the integration of all Portuguese into a single national movement (Pais 9 May 1918).

Another charge that has often been laid at the door of Sidónio's regime was that it was a type of fascism *avante le letter* (Martins 1968: 309; Schwartzman 1989; Duarte 1942; Pais 1980; Villaverde Cabral 1980), in much the same way that Napoleon III's Second Empire is regarded as a 19th-century precursor of 20th-century fascism.[19]

The contention Sidónio was a fascist is normally advanced on the basis his regime combined several of the aspects that were to be found in 1930s Italy: a single party; a charismatic leader; populist demonstrations; organic political representation (corporatism); and a political and social ideology that combined a yearning for the past with a desire for economic modernisation.[20] However, there are those who deny Sidónio was a fascist, arguing the mixture of ideals in his project can be found in all conservative authoritarian regimes (Telo 1998: 24).[21]

Without wishing to become embroiled in a debate over what does and does not constitute fascism, we must accept that as the charge has been made it must be investigated.

To investigate Sidonismo as some sort of pre-fascism, we must first define what is meant by fascism and how it compares to Sidonismo.

Recognising fascism is 'probably the vaguest of contemporary political terms' (Payne 1980: 4) we are always going to be left with a problem defining what is meant by it.

There are at least two sets of criteria that have been proposed as a means through which it is possible to determine if a regime is fascist.

The first of these is Nolte's six point 'fascist minimum',[22] which while apparently simplistic is an attempt to systematise the concept of fascism and distinguish it from other right-wing regimes.[23]

Payne (1980: 6-7) develops Nolte's minima by adding into the mix the idea that the interwar fascist movements were concerned with 'a new set of common negations, aspects of a new formal style, somewhat normal modes of organisation, and... a new orientation in political culture and ideology'.

According to Payne, while it is necessary to identify the fascist negations, the presence or absence of these are not sufficient grounds on which to attribute or refuse to attribute the label fascist.

Before this can be done, an investigation must

be made into the movement's positive ideals—that is, its goals, as well as its organisation and organisational style.

By adopting Payne's criteria, it becomes very difficult to attribute the fascist label to either Sidónio or his regime.

Rather than looking towards Mussolini's Fascist Italy for comparisons with Sidónio's New Republic, one would be better employed looking towards Primo de Rivera's Spain (1923-30).

Both Iberian dictators came from similar upper-class provincial backgrounds, they were both rather dashing military figures with a history of political involvement, they both followed similar 'intuitionist' policies designed both to maintain their popularity and ensure continued social peace and economic development and neither had any prior involvement in left-wing politics.[24]

The New Republic

Although the New Republic did not come into official existence until the elections of April 1918, for several reasons, not least of which are clarity and simplicity, here we will define it as having existed from the date the Democratic regime was finally overthrown (8 December 1917) until the outbreak of civil war following the Santarém Uprising on 11 January 1919 that led to the declaration of the Monarchy of the North in Porto by the Northern Military Junta eight days later.

Is it reasonable to assume the Sidonista regime was, from the outset, determined to defend a republican solution?

There are several reasons why it is reasonable to make this assumption.

First, with regards Sidónio Pais, he was at pains throughout his brief reign to emphasise his republican credentials, as he made clear during a speech to the 20th Infantry Regiment in Guimarães on 14 January 1918, at a time his acceptance of monarchist support was being exploited by supporters of the ousted regime:

> They also mention that monarchists have entered the 5 December movement. Yes, they have joined, but not as monarchists. They are honest men, incapable of doing what is said of them.

> It is enough to note that at the head of the government stands a man who has been a Republican since he was 15 years old and that Machado Santos is a member of the Revolutionary Junta, and that other well-known Republicans are ministers of the new regime to understand that there will be no betrayal. They may say what they like and convince those who will be convinced, but the government is republican and will never do anything to betray the Republic. I make this affirmation so that there can be no doubts and declare that this Republic will seek to recognise all citizens as Portuguese and will respect their beliefs.

The following day, at a banquet at the Central Hotel in Viana do Castelo, this position was restated with equal force:

> I confirm once more my republican convictions and refute all those who would allege that I am playing a game with the monarchists that will open the way for a monarchical restoration. I have been a Republican since I was 15 years old. The founder of the Republic, Machado Santos, is a member of my government, as are other Republicans. I have never betrayed, nor will I ever betray, my Republican faith and principles… As

> a Republican I will oppose implacably
> any attempt to restore the monarchy.

His repeated protestations of his resolute belief in republicanism were noted by his monarchist supporters who, while perhaps not wishing to believe his resolve, nonetheless accepted that with Sidónio at the helm the path to restoration was blocked.

Faced with Sidónio's intransigence regarding the regime question, the Integralists, who were his most consistent monarchist supporters, instead adapted their own beliefs to the new situation (Braga da Cruz 1980; 1986; Raposo 1945).

Seeking to guide the new regime towards their preferred outcome, which was primarily to prevent the re-emergence of the Democratic regime—that is, to foil any repeat of the events of May 1915,[25] they aligned themselves with Sidónio, whose 'mentality, still deformed by strong connections to and sympathies for Jacobinism, could not envisage other lines or other plans for reform that did not seem to lead to the repetition of the errors that he was seeking to remedy' (Raposo 1945: 36).

By January 1918, the Integralists recognised that the first phase of Sidónio's coup was complete and that it was time to develop a programme for the institutionalisation of the new regime: 'It was now necessary to innovate, to reform, to substitute what was destroyed or appeared to be destroyed by the words of the victorious proclamations. It was under these circumstances that it fell to Integralismo Lusitano to inspire and to collaborate' (Raposo 1945: 36).

While being pro-Republican, Sidónio's pronouncements did in most other respects mirror the concerns that had been developed and discussed by Integralism since its foundation in 1914.

For example, during a speech at Viana do Castelo on 15 January 1918, Sidónio spoke of the need 'to end the hatred that divides the Portuguese family', a message that was reinforced in an interview published in Diário Nacional when he stated that:

> We have freed the country from the Democratic oligarchy, replacing it with a government of freedom and morality. We have already done much. There remains much to be done. What is it that we seek to do? To reconcile the Portuguese family!

To the Integralists, such statements were proof Sidónio was worthy of support, possibly in the hope that he could be persuaded to accept their programme in its entirety.

Sardinha, who was elected as a monarchist deputy for the town of Elvas in the legislative elections of April 1918, was not averse to making a direct comparison between the integralist doctrine, of which he was the main author, and the policies being implemented by the regime, as is clear in his statement of support for Sidonismo:

> We are giving him our complete loyalty... Sidónio Pais is making an interesting demonstration of Integralism in this country (Medina 1978: 73).

This 'interesting demonstration' was, according to Costa Pinto (1994: 31) largely the result of Sidónio 'adopting some of their programmatic objectives into his ideas for corporatist representation', a consequence, suggests Telo (1998: 24), of his regime lacking any ideological programme of his own.[26]

The idea that Sidónio's regime lacked a coherent ideological programme of its own and that it was forced to adopt many of the proposals suggested by the Integralists has a certain validity.

As we have seen, all the pronouncements made by the revolutionaries in the days and weeks immediately following the coup mentioned only the need to overthrow the *Democratic oligarchy* and *restore justice and the rule of law,*[27] *secure order,*[28] *maintain order, ensure the rule of law and demand respect for life and property,*[29] *reintegrate the Republic in its purity,* [30]*for the New Republic, for order,*[31] and so on.

What is absent from all of these pronouncements is the slightest hint of a programme outlining how these objectives were to be achieved, although given the heterogeneous and soft nature of the regime's initial support, it is not unreasonable to assume that even had a programme existed, it would have been prudent for the regime not to publicise the details—for that is where the devil lies and where the support may have been lost.[32]

It should not come as a surprise to discover Integralism sought to fashion the New Republic in its own image, especially since it is true that Integralism was the only group that had developed any kind of ideological strategy or doctrinal theory during the Republic.

Since Sidónio had made it clear from a very early stage that he sought the rebirth of the Republic—that he aimed to create the Republic that had been promised on 5 October rather than the one that had been delivered—it was obvious that none of the proposals made by the Republican politicians who had been responsible for the betrayed Republic could be acceptable.

While there were degrees of guilt to be attributed to each individual Republican party, with Afonso Costa's Democrats being the chief demons, what was certain was that the politicians in the remaining factions, including Brito Camacho's Unionists, shared some of the responsibility and therefore some of the guilt.

This would then explain Sidónio's declaration that his regime would 'accept all honest and well-intentioned men without regard to their political creed or to their religion' (Pais 15 January 1918).

Honest and well-intentioned to the extent that they genuinely wished to see a new Portugal rise from the ashes of the old, and regardless of their politics and religion to the degree that they were willing to set aside sectarian views and embrace and support the moves to 'reconcile the Portuguese family'.

While this effectively excluded the majority of the *historic* Republicans, the emphasis on republican renewal and the deliberate association of the *old* Republic with the constitutional monarchy, effectively ruled out any role, certainly any significant role, for the Constitutionalists in the development of the new regime's programme.[33]

Despite their contribution to the regime's programme, Sidónio's commitment to Republicanism was sufficient to prevent the Integralists from participating in the single party that was being set up under the leadership of Egaz Moniz.

While the Integralists did not 'profess the legitimacy of the king as a person, but proclaimed the legitimacy of the national interest: we are nationalists before we are monarchists' (Raposo cited in Braga da Cruz 1982: 114), its continuing commitment to the Republic meant Sidonismo 'lacked a basis in history that is the fundamental truth of monarchies' (Raposo cited in Medina 1978: 74).

The Integralists also refused to accept official positions within the regime, preferring instead to collaborate from behind the scenes.

So it was that Pequito Rebelo could work on proposals for agricultural reform while also refusing to accept appointment to head the General Commission on Agriculture 'on account of his being a monarchist and thus being unable to accept positions of confidence within the Republic, even when it is led by Sidónio, a man of such intelligence and morality' (Raposo 1945: 38).

Raposo, who was a middle-ranking civil servant at this time, claims that he turned down Martinho Nobre de Melo's offer of a more senior position within the Justice Ministry,[34] because 'we are in a Republic, and I am a monarchist... Consequently, I live independently and owe no favours to regime that I believe it is my political duty to oppose' (Raposo 1945: 40).

In an unambiguous reference to Sidonismo, António Sardinha explained why the Integralist collaboration was not to extend to formal Integralist participation: 'Presidentialism is absurd as it lacks all continuity. Despite being genial, Napoleon also fell' (Sardinha 5 July 1918, cited in Medina 1978: 74).

The new regime's relations with the organised Catholic Church were also far from straightforward.

While the Church welcomed the positive noises

coming from the new political rulers about a form of separation that was on the Church's terms, it did not believe the regime was going far enough to reverse the worst effects of the 1911 Law of Separation.

The Church's main complaint was the lay committees established by the Democrats to manage Church affairs at the local level were to be left intact, although given the new interpretations of the laws governing the Church's function within Portuguese society, there can be little doubt these lay committees would be less intrusive in matters of religious practice.[35]

Yet, despite the new and less hostile climate, the Church authorities remained determined to retain their political independence with respect to the state and its representatives.

As far as the Church was concerned, the best defence was still separation. Its favoured relationship with Sidónio's regime was one of partnership in which both parties would remain independent but supportive of one another.

The benefits of this were obvious: first, by refusing to incorporate itself into the regime, the Church was ensuring it could not be accused of manipulating the political system—a charge that had been laid against it by the Republicans during the constitutional monarchy and provided the justification for the Law of Separation; second, the regime also benefited to the extent that it became more difficult to realistically accuse it of being subject to clerical domination, a fact that enabled it to maintain its appeal with those Republicans who, while perhaps not anti-clerical, nonetheless remained suspicious of the Church hierarchy.

Considering its function to run in parallel with the regime, the Church authorities refused to allow their political organisation, the Catholic Centre, from participating in Sidónio's single party, preferring instead to issue its own manifesto on 14 March 1918, which called on 'all men of true faith and vehement patriotism, without distinction or the need to sacrifice their political ideals, to introduce into public life the Christian values of justice and charity and to demand and defend the rights and liberties of the Church' (Actualidade 28 March 1918).[36]

This document also explained the Church's attitude towards the new regime, making clear its support for Sidónio while also warning that this support was not unconditional and that it could not be taken for granted:

> The honest part of the country demonstrated—by more significant means than an electoral consultation—that it would give its support to whoever can guarantee it order, honest and patriotic administration, respect for beliefs and the right to exercise legitimate liberties. With respect to religious freedoms,

> some demonstrations of goodwill have already been made towards the Catholics and the promise has been made that they will reform that odious and iniquitous law that for seven years has been declared a keystone and intangible safeguard, the so-called Law of Separation that has served only as an instrument of expropriation and oppression. We have seen the promised reforms. However, by a lamentable contradiction, they do not correspond to our expectations, nor are they a reflection of the just proposals made by the Head of State (*Actualidade* 28 March 1918).

The Catholics did not limit their demands to the abolition of the 1911 law. They also sought the re-establishment of diplomatic relations with the Holy See,[37] and a revision of the constitution.[38]

To ensure the regime remained committed to these goals, the Catholic Centre believed it would be better for Catholics to supervise the regime rather than become a part of it.

While they advocated 'Catholics vote for Sidónio Pais in the presidential election', they also declared that 'where our organisation allows us to present a Centre candidate, then one must be presented' in the legislative elections (*Actualidade* 28 March 1918).

While the integralists and the Catholics were prepared to extend qualified support to the New

Republic, the old Republican parties were not. For obvious reasons, the Democratic Party was deliberately excluded. José de Almeida's Evolutionists were also demonised by the new regime, principally on account of their participation in the Sacred Union government of April 1916 to April 1917 and then for their activities during the summer and autumn of 1917, when they supported Afonso Costa's attempts to prevent a parliamentary inquiry into the alleged atrocities committed by the army in Africa (Ribeiro de Meneses 1998b).

The exclusion of these two Republican groups left Brito Camacho's Unionists and a small group of disillusioned former Evolutionists who had broken from the party in late 1916 and coalesced into a new party, the Centrists, under the leadership of Egaz Moniz in September 1917.

A third grouping of disenchanted Republicans were led by the symbolic father of the Republic and commander of Republican troops in Lisbon on 5 October 1910, Machado Santos.

This last group was perhaps the most idealistic of all and was a long standing opponent of the Democratic republican oligarchy.

Machado Santos, the *hero of the Rotunda,* had already rebelled against the Republic on 13 December 1916 (Medeiros Ferreira 1992: 58-60) and maintained his opposition to the 'continuation of the vicious circle in which we live: the permanent existence of democratic parliamentary majorities elected by cliques which, in turn, obliged the formation of cabinets created to provide "jobs for the boys"' (Farelo Lopes 1994: 66).

Sidónio's campaign against the parliamentary Republic was designed to incorporate the Unionist Party 'which had done everything within the law to end the shameful acts of parliamentarism' (Pais 17 February 1918).

The development of Sidonismo's political programme, particularly the decision to create a single party,[39] and the declaration of support for a presidential list system of government, with the president elected in a national plebiscite, which was announced on 17 February 1918,[40] caused Camacho and the Unionists to reconsider their support for the New Republic 'and to minimise their involvement in raising Pais to power' (Ribeiro de Meneses 1998b: 116).

In his several public pronouncements, Sidónio stressed the need for national unity and for an end to the strife of party politics.

This was the public motivation behind the creation of the National Republican Party (PNR).

This party was intended to incorporate 'all good Portuguese' and help undermine the parties of the previous regime.

Led by Egaz Moniz, and including several former Unionists, Evolutionists, *machadistas* and a disparate collection of individuals with no prior party affiliations, the PNR was formed in the belief that 'the people are not merely the crowd, the brute total, but rather the nation organised in families, communes, districts and provinces' (*Diário do Governo* 30 March 1918).

To encourage a sense of organic community, the PNR was given extensive organisational resources and almost complete control of the state legislative apparatus.

However, the decision of the *historic* Republican parties to boycott the new organisation, combined with the decision by the Integralists and Catholics to organise separately, undermined the PNR, with the result that it became 'simply another party', albeit a highly privileged one (Ribeiro de Meneses 199b: 116).

By August 1918, it was becoming clear the PNR's lack of a guiding doctrine and its inability to generate any real popular support was leaving it vulnerable to opposition groupings both inside and outside parliament.

On 9 August, Moniz wrote to Sidónio warning him that despite its domination of the legislature elected in April the party was on the verge of collapse.

The need to create a movement that could foster a sense of national unity was also important to the developmental aspect of Sidónio's project, which was initially restricted to resolving the political question and the restoration of order.[41]

Table 1: Deputies elected to the Legislative Assembly

Grouping	Deputies	%
PNR	108	69.7
Monarchists	37	23.9
Catholics	5	3.2
Independents	5	3.2

Source: Oliveira Marques (1975), Farelo Lopes (1994)

Throughout Sidónio's time in power his regime never managed to progress beyond the political question, and at no time was an attempt made to introduce economic programmes that could alter the system inherited from the liberal regime.

Ultimately, this can be seen as a sign of Sidónio's failure, as he was never to achieve a position from which he could forge the economic support structures for his New Republic.

Instead, he could only try to use his undoubted popular support to cajole the important social and economic groups into accepting his political programme—one that did not threaten the material interests of these groups.

The proposals for a strong presidential a system supported by a powerful executive authority and a weak legislature could even be advantageous for these groups, which could exercise influence over the regime.

This alone is sufficient to explain the regime's rapid loss of legitimacy and control during the summer and autumn of 1918, as the various social groups began to withdraw their support and to advance their own programmes for the future political and economic settlement.[42]

It was Sidónio's inability to promote a programme that could incorporate all the disparate elements of his initial support that led to the failure of the PNR as a political movement.

One of the problems facing the regime party was that it was formed after the fact—as a reaction to a situation it was intended to maintain.

The need to unite diverse and heterogeneous forces was immediately supplemented by the requirement for the party to develop an ideology that would be sufficiently vague as to be inclusive, while also developing adequate resources of authority to ensure compliance with this same ideology.

That the PNR patently failed to do so was the inevitable consequence of the regime's failure to recognise that 'legitimacy and acquiescence and legitimacy and consensus are not the same' (Freidrich cited in Schaar 1981: 21) and that the 'acquiescent' legitimacy the regime enjoyed during its first few months was born out of a negative reaction to the one it had succeeded.

To secure its position, regardless of Sidónio's charismatic appeal, the PNR would have had to create a consensus around the Sidonista project, something it was unable to do as long as that project itself could not overcome the centrifugal forces operating within it.[43]

The failure of the PNR was put into sharp relief by the decision of the three key groups not to participate within it, with the Integralists and Catholics deciding to contest the legislative elections of 28 April 1918 in opposition to the regime party, and Brito Camacho's Unionists deciding to boycott the elections altogether by joining Afonso Costa's Democrats and Almeida's Evolutionists in opposition to the regime.[44]

While the failure of the PNR to successfully establish itself as a single party may have been a direct consequence of its inability to develop a doctrinal programme capable of uniting all sections of non-Democratic Portuguese society, this failure remains to be explained in the light of Sidónio's personal popularity.

Similarly, as Manuel de Lucena (1994) and Linz (1973: 172n1) have pointed out, the initial absence of a coherent political programme is not necessarily a barrier to a regime's ability to develop a coherent set of political priorities—rather it can be an advantage while it is attempting to legitimise its rule by permitting it to appeal to a wider and potentially disloyal audience.[45]

Essentially, it can buy some time for a regime

that emerged without the support of an identifiable movement to institutionalise its hold on power through, for example, the establishment of a legitimacy that is not dependent upon generally accepted concepts of legal succession.[46]

Telo (1998) and Ribeiro de Meneses (1998b) adopt the position that Sidónio's purpose all along had been to secure a mandate in his own person and that the creation of the single party should be regarded as an example of his pragmatic approach to government.

Telo believes that during the first few weeks of the regime, Sidonismo evolved from a movement seeking the support of the anti-Democratic republicans into a regime that was structured in response to the social and political problems that had emerged outside of parliament.

Sidonismo was forced to integrate all shades of opinion, including monarchist opinion, into its programme.

The PNR was created to be a vehicle through which the expression of these opinions could be institutionalised and controlled while Sidónio set about the task of establishing his own separate constituency through direct appeals to the people.

The fact Sidónio was not the leader of the PNR, a task that fell to the 'historic' figure of Egaz Moniz, is crucial to understanding the role the party was to play in Sidónio's project.

Sidónio professed his support for the concept of a single party of *bons portugueses* (good Portuguese), while keeping this party at arm's length.

The PNR could serve to unite wealthy sectors and create an efficient system of favoured distribution while also operating as a channel for political discussion; and if it succeeded in this essentially demobilisational task, Sidónio was able to accept the credit for success while being in a position to deny all responsibility for failure.

While Ribeiro de Meneses (1998b: 117) advises us to treat with caution Teófilo Duarte's claim the PNR was never intended to be anything other than a 'smokescreen preparing public opinion for a new presidentialist corporatist dictatorship', he goes on to make almost the same point when he states: 'What was important was the personality cult'.

His reservations regarding the extension of the franchise, the creation of party newspapers and the parliamentary composition of the PNR seem easily explained in the context of the creation of a personality cult that would provide Sidónio with charismatic legitimacy, which is defined by Weber as:

> ...a devotion to the exceptional sanctity, heroism or exemplary character of an individual person and of the normative

> patterns of order revealed or ordained by him (cited in Connolly 1984: 8).

Taking each of Ribeiro de Meneses's reservations into account, we can easily demonstrate the PNR was an important instrument in the establishment of Sidónio's personal legitimacy.

The extension of the franchise, even for the legislative elections, was important for several reasons.

First, by denouncing the oligarchical practises of the previous regime, Sidónio had criticised the Democratic Party's electoral machinery that had maintained and institutionalised the clientelistic system of the constitutional monarchy.

Sidónio understood this network of Democratic *caciques* had not been destroyed by the removal of the Democratic Party from power and that it represented a very real threat to his position.

However, he was also aware that by cutting off the head, the body would wither over time, and that the only sure way to prevent the resurgence of these networks, given their tradition of situationism, was to offer them a position within the new regime.[47]

Sidónio, though, was unwilling to permit the *caciques* to openly exploit their power, which could have resulted in the early return of the Democrats, as happened in May 1915 following the overthrow of Pimenta de Castro's dictatorship.

The franchise was a blunt instrument in this

respect. A large electorate could not on its own break the hold of the *caciques* and, whatever the regime's public statements to the contrary, this was not the intention.

The objective in enlarging the franchise was essentially twofold. Subjectively, given the importance a restricted franchise played in the maintenance and internal logic of Democratic Party rule (Farelo Lopes 1994), its enlargement was a potent weapon in the propaganda battle against supporters of the ousted regime.

The idea of a larger electorate was significant for several reasons. Positively, it was a carrot dangled in front of previously excluded groups, promising them the right of participation and the ability to help in the creation of a new order, and allowing them to integrate into that order.

Negatively, the promise of integration appealed to those who had been excluded by the Democrats, giving them the power to prevent their return.

This also served as an appeal to the subjective perceptions of those elite groups that had lost their political influence during the liberal Republic—especially the Catholics and monarchists, but also the urban working classes and the rural peasantry: social groups that had never exercised political power, and political influence only intermittently.

The propagandistic promise was that the new political authorities would allow their voices to be heard in the new Portugal that was being constructed, a goal that was stated unambiguously by Sidónio in a speech at Santarém on 4 March 1918:

> The government that emerged from the Edward VII Park has as its goal the union of all Portuguese spirits in order to achieve the resurgence of our country... If the party organisations were the heirs to the activistic defects of monarchism, then it is important that they do not continue. We need to follow another path, one that will take us away from sectarianism.

The new party was to be an instrument in this attempt to deal with the political question, the problem that Sidónio believed was foremost in the minds of the Portuguese people.

To overcome these subjective fears, Sidónio emphasised the role of the single party as a force that could mobilise opinion against the reappearance of the 'forces of calumny, of intrigue and of conspiracy',[48] by 'uniting as one to ensure our victory'.[49]

Objectively, however, the PNR and the extended franchise served an altogether different purpose, one that was designed to appeal to the political *caciques* and persuade them to join in the revolution.

The success of this latter depended primarily on the popular acceptance of the former and the subsequent weakening of the PNR's power. Sidónio was aware of the dangers inherent in allowing the PNR to develop its own popular constituency and of granting it any real role in the government of the country.

The extended franchise, combined with the PNR's virtual monopoly of the available political space ensured the party would emerge as the dominant political formation, thus serving its propagandist purpose.

To understand the true nature of Sidónio's plans, we must examine the role the party was allowed to pursue within his regime, and it was very far removed from the one implied in his public pronouncements.

Sidónio did not appear troubled by the decision of Brito Camacho to lead his party out of the new regime.

Indeed, this desertion provided him with more ammunition in his propaganda campaign against the Democrats, dismissing it out of hand with a simple remark: 'They may say what they like, but those who at this moment oppose the government are with the Democrats'.[50]

To serve its objective purpose and to encourage the *caciques* to throw in their lot with the New Republic, Sidónio had to demonstrate the PNR, especially with its popular mandate, did not represent any threat.

Camacho obviously recognised this was the real goal, prompting him to withdraw his support once it became clear Sidónio did not intend his regime to be merely a *regime d'exception* prompted by the exigencies of war (Medeiros Ferreira 1992: 72).

While it may be argued the decision to reserve one-third of the seats in the new legislature for minority parties reflected Sidónio's desire towards inclusiveness (Ribeiro de Meneses 1998b: 117-8), there can be little doubt it also served to undermine the PNR's role as a single party, as it invited the creation of parties in opposition to it.

This left the door open for the monarchists and the Catholics to organise independently of the PNR, ensuring the legislature would be divided.

This appears to have been a deliberate tactic on Sidónio's part, as it presented the appearance of national integration while ensuring the PNR was distracted by the need to compete for electoral support at the same time as it had to develop a political doctrine that would distinguish it from the electoral opposition.

The PNR was operating in a doctrinal no-man's land, with political space being left open for those groups that had either developed their own doctrinal programmes, such as the Integralists, or that had retained their own pre-liberal regime views, for example, the Catholics, the constitutional monarchists, the Legitimists and, on a much smaller scale, the socialists. With the desertion of the Unionists back into the Democratic camp, the PNR was forced to direct its appeal towards the political elites in the hope it could attract men capable of developing a positive programme and thereby neglecting the newly enfranchised masses (Ribeiro de Meneses 1998b: 118).

This lifted the immediate threat to the political *caciques*.

Another important role allocated to the PNR, and one that also served the dual purpose described above,[51] was to promote the Sidónio personality cult.

The party was provided with a network of newspapers throughout the country in a determined effort to ensure the message would be tailored to suit the audience.

Armed with this weapon, the PNR set about promoting Sidónio in almost divine terms, as this example from the first edition of *O Norte* illustrates:

> Sidónio Pais is one of those figures whom destiny singled out to come forth at decisive points in the history of a people, to save and redeem it (22 April 1918).

The image of Sidónio painted by the PNR press is that of a 'heroic man of action and deed' (Ribeiro de Meneses 1998b: 118) who is willing to sacrifice his life for the good of the motherland.

The PNR media was an important tool in developing this image of Sidónio, expanding upon his own statements and activities, imbuing them with the necessary traits of selflessness—his heroism in personally leading government forces against a naval revolt in January 1918 and the fact he travelled the country without a bodyguard—these were all described in messianic terms designed deliberately to contrast with the intrinsic modesty of Sidónio's own statements and his own self-promotion as a reluctant hero.

'No one desires my death more than I' (Castro 1923: 23), one example of Sidónio's discourse remembered five years after his death that speaks to the power of the PNR's machine. It could take extracts from Sidónio's pronouncements and imbue them with messianic significance and isolate him from the failure to alter the Portuguese mentality:

> The mental and moral incapacity of the people selected to lead and the special phenomenon of the conflict between the Republic and the monarchy cancelled out the immediate implementation of his work. Imprisoned by republican and restorationist preconceptions, the nation did not organise organically... Past divisions were renewed and the political conflicts began once more (Castro 1923: 32).

Absolved of any blame, Sidónio could be promoted

as the epitome of selflessness. Thus, the significance of this external propaganda cannot be overstated,[52] for it created a legacy that continued long after Sidónio's assassination and the collapse of his regime. The importance of the PNR press was precisely in this—to create the cult of Sidónio—the development of political debate was kept within these bounds, at the 'meta' level, and was never allowed to 'descend' to the mere detail.

Sidónio's regime bore more than a passing resemblance to the Second French Empire of Napoleon III. The absence of any formal constitutional settlement in the New Republic did not weaken his position, at least in the short term,[53] as it allowed him to play the competing factions off against one another.

While he made it clear he had no intention of allowing a monarchical restoration,[54] his non-movement on the question of the constitution gave the monarchists, and especially the Integralists, cause to pause—for they were all aware the only alternatives to Sidónio were either a civil war that would in all probability lead to the return of the Democrats,[55] or the immediate return of the Democrats and all that entailed, particularly given their belief Sidonismo was failing to engender the new man fit for the new republic:

> Political messianism died or will die in an epileptic fury within the parties

> where it still lives... The legitimate creators of hope cannot be the genius or the will of one man, it cannot come from the generous proposals of a group or a faction: Portugal, conscious of its own reality, must provide its own salvation through the coordination and the harmonisation of its chosen values (Raposo cited in Braga da Cruz 1986: 46-7).

What Sidónio could buy them was the time they needed to spread their message in the knowledge that he 'overcame the effects of democratic and discipline but left their causes intact.

Sidõnio's government represented a reaction against the 'Democratic anarchy that jealously guards its fountain of poison' (Almeida Braga 1943: 48-9), and while it clearly did not represent the solution to the political question, at least as far as the Integralists were concerned, Sidonismo did mark a step in the direction towards some semblance of a restoration of order.

Appendix:
The structure of Portuguese industry in 1917

	Unit size by number of employees			
	<10	11-250	251-1000	>1000
Quarrying	46	26	0	0
Metallurgy	602	174	8	0
Ceramics	116	69	2	0
Glass	2	12	3	1
Chemicals	75	44	4	0
Food	656	354	7	0
Textiles	134	292	37	2
Clothing	286	88	1	0
Footwear	305	64	0	0
Skins	103	55	0	0
Construction	47	8	0	0
Furniture	784	256	4	0
Paper	15	23	1	0
Graphics	148	71	1	0
Art	142	45	0	0
Tobacco	0	0	3	1
Electricity	15	6	1	0
Distribution	150	26	0	0
Special Industries	81	25	0	0
Land Transport	23	4	0	1
Other	26	32	2	1
Total	3756	1674	74	6
%	68.17	30.38	1.34	0.11

Source: Boletim de Trabalho Industrial, 116 (Medeiros 1978: 75)

	Number of employees			
Total	Male	Female	Children	Total
72	1251	97	99	1447
784	9410	379	1895	11751
187				4021
18				2887
123				3745
1017	10261	8868	3104	24601
465	11583	16645	6786	36124
375				5298
369				2627
158				1876
55				346
1044	10328	1324	2011	13950
39				2558
220				3017
187				1080
4				3316
22				497
176				1257
106				1179
28				2288
61	837	198	140	4199
5510	43670	27511	14035	128054
100.00				

Notes

[1] The entry of the US into the war during 1917 resulted in the diversion of transport ships and their warship escorts from Lisbon and Africa to the North Atlantic where they were required to bring US troops and their supplies to France. Discontent within the Expeditionary Corps (CEP), which had broken into the open with Machado Santos' revolt in December 1916, several weeks before the first troops were scheduled to embark, continued throughout the war, perhaps reaching a peak in late 1917 with the publication and distribution of a pamphlet, *Rol de Deshonra,* dated 5 September and which was produced anonymously and distributed by troops serving in the CEP in France. This document was a thinly veiled attack on Afonso Costa's Democrats.

[2] Schwartzman adopts Prezworski's thesis that democracy consists of a 'social compromise among classes that have inherently conflicting interests' and develops this to incorporate the notion these compromises are given form through a series of formal and informal pacts, of which an example may be a political party. These parts, she suggests, may be horizontal—that is, between different interest groups—or vertical—between social classes (1989: 176-7).

[3] According to Payne, there were 2500 factories in Lisbon, employing 65,000 people, an average of 26 per factory, while in Porto 364 factories employed 26,000 people, giving it an average factory size of 71 employees.

[4] In September 1917 War Minister Norton de Matos introduced a decree law that made striking postal workers subject to military discipline.

[5] Egaz Moniz had been a member of the Evolutionist Party until 1916 when he and some others left in protest José de Almeida's decision to lead the party into the Sacred Union government. In 1917 he formed the Centrist Party which, along with Camacho's Unionist Party, formed the core of the Parliamentary Bloc that acted as an opposition to Afonso Costa's government until its overthrow by Sidónio. For more on the centrist party see Oliveira Marques (1975), for more on the Parliamentary Bloc and its tactics during the secret parliamentary sessions of July 1917, see Ribeiro de Meneses (1998a). For the relationship between the Centrists and the Unionists on the eve of Sidónio's coup, see the satirical newspaper, *Os Ridículos,* especially the edition dated 30 October 1917.

[6] Farelo Lopes (1994) describes a process through which high-profile members, the political bosses or *caciques,* of non-republican parties and movements declared their adherence to the new republican regime. In

many cases, this was proclaimed in local newspapers. The transfer of support by the *caciques* was invariably followed by their entire political networks. This process, he shows, was repeated in virtually all provinces and municipalities.

[7] Because the 1911 Electoral Law did not explicitly deny women the vote, one woman doctor was able to demand enrolment and was permitted to vote in the 1911 legislative elections. See Farelo Lopes (1972: 135).

[8] The previous electoral law, established on 28 March 1895 by Hinz Ribeiro, was specifically designed to weaken the Republicans in their strongholds, particularly in Lisbon, through alterations to electoral boundaries and the introduction of tax qualifications in addition to the already established literacy qualifications. The introduction of this law prompted the Republican Party to abstain from the elections of 17 November 1895 as part of its campaign to call the legitimacy of the monarchist regime into question.

[9] See Oliveria Marques (1975: 57). 'The majority of men in Portugal as throughout the Latin world did not practice religion. Religion was a thing for women'.

[10] Although Wheeler (1972) argues the military's role in the October Revolution has been exaggerated, claiming most of the units stationed in Lisbon remained neutral (1972: 182), as did those outside the capital (1972: 185). He believes the main reason the army has been considered central to the success of the revolution was the fact that 'in the final phase of the ritual, crowds of *populares* cheered the army units for remaining neutral and for adhering to the Republic... The revolutionary hero of the Rotunda, Machado Santos, later wrote that the victory of the Republic in 1910 was really the victory of the people' (1972: 186). Schwartzman (1989: 33) calculates the size of the pro-Republican armed forces at 450 'including the Navy, the infantry and the artillery', although she does not state how she reaches this figure.

[11] See Wheeler (1972) for an alternative view that attributes the Republican victory to the support of the Lisbon working class.

[12] Costa Pinto (1998: 4-6) shows how the Democratic Party preferred to use the patronage power of the state and limited suffrage to ensure a workable compromise between its urban middle-class supporters and the 'key provincial notables' who guaranteed the operation of the clientelist network. The compromise between urban and rural sectors was, he argues, ensured through the governmentalisation of local administration in which state-appointed district governors sustained the clientelistic pacts, thereby ensuring Democratic victory in rural areas.

[13] See Hermano Neves, *Como Triunfou a República*, Lisbon: Empreza Liberdade (1910).

[14] *Enfiteuse* was a form of feudal title granted to peasants in exchange for payments, either in kind or in money. Many landowners exploited the system as a form of social control, as the feuars' title could be withdrawn at any time and under any pretext through, for example, increases in the land burdens imposed on feuars who did not follow the landowner's instructions. The abolition of *enfiteuse* resulted in the transfer of title to the feuar.

[15] A not unimportant sector, given that 83% of the population in 1911 lived in rural communities (Oliveira Marques Max1975:127).

[16] There was a marked increase in the military's political importance dating from 1910. In addition to Pimenta de Castro's coup of 1915, there were also examples of military actions designed to influence government policy. One such example was Machado Santos's revolt of December 1916 in protest at the imminent embarkation of troops for France. The ten months that passed between Portugal's official entry into the war on 9 March 1916 and the first troop embarkations in January 1917 have been seen as an example of the military's increasingly political role (Medeiros Ferreira 1992), as has the Democratic Party's refusal to allow a parliamentary inquiry into alleged atrocities against the native populations of Angola and Mozambique in 1916 (Ribeiro de Meneses 1998b).

[17] Or more particularly, the failures of the Democratic Party led by Afonso Costa.

[18] Proclamation of the Revolutionary Committee, 8 December 1917. Signed by Sidónio Pais, Machado Santos and Feliciano da Costa.

[19] Plessis (1987 [1979]: 6) reproduces a lengthy extract from Vaussard's *Histoire de L'Italie Moderne* (Paris 1950) comparing Napoleon III with Mussolini: 'Both men, in the wake of a social crisis that set proletarian expectations aflame in a wild and disorderly fashion, frightened the bourgeoisie and laid the groundwork for the exercise of personal rule, took advantage of the impotence of elected assemblies to acquire—with the extensive connivance of the military, financial and certain aristocratic circles—the acquiescence of the majority in a coup d'etat dressed up as a return to order'. Many of these same charges have been laid against Sidónio and his regime.

[20] For a discussion of Italian Fascism's developmental nature, see A. J. Gregor, *Italian Fascism and Developmental Dictatorship*, Princeton, NJ: LPE (1979). Gregor's discussion (1979: 134-6) of Alfredo Rocco's

views on industrial development are particularly pertinent. Telo (1998: 19-23) describes Sidónio's project in terms that align almost perfectly with the plans advanced by Rocco.

[21] Telo (1998: 19-23) identifies seven key elements in Sidonismo that are also present in other right-wing dictatorships: patriotism, charismatic leadership, tendency to overcome political divisions, understanding of the state's role in society, a new concept of democracy, recognition that parties are not the perfect form of representation, and a belief in traditional values.

[22] The six minima are: anti-Marxism, anti-liberalism, anti-conservatism, the leadership principle, a party army, and the aim of totalitarianism (Nolte 1968 cited in Payne 1980: 5-6).

[23] Payne criticises Nolte for deriving his model from German National Socialism and, therefore, not amenable to broader comparisons with the Latin world.

[24] For more on Primo de Rivera's regime, see Ben-Ami (1979) and Carr (1968).

[25] General Pimenta de Castro came to power in January 1915 at the invitation of President Arriaga and with the support of conservative Republicans and monarchists. During his time in office, he attempted to create a new political system that would prevent domination by the Democrats. However, in May 1915 a popular revolution in Lisbon led to the restoration of the Democratic Party.

[26] Telo says Sidónio was a 'mere' apprentice when it came to governing, and that while he was a Republican and a democrat by conviction, he was obliged by circumstances to accept monarchist support and to abandon his own desires. He believes Sidónio was little more than a 'charismatic pragmatist' whose regime gradually moved from seeking the support of anti-Democratic Republicans into one that was structured in response to social and political problems that were independent of the parliamentary and party systems (1998: 24). Such an analysis bears more than a passing resemblance to Carr's (1966) description of Primo de Rivera's 1923-30 dictatorship in neighbouring Spain and seems to deny the suggestion Sidónio was a Portuguese Bonaparte.

[27] Supplement No 1, *Diário do Governo*, 8 December 1917.

[28] Supplement No 2, *Diário do Governo*, 8 December 1917.

[29] Undated proclamation of the Revolutionary Junta, signed by Sidónio Pais, Machado Santos and Feliciano da Costa.

[30] Sidónio's speech on taking office as Foreign Minister, 12 December 1917.

[31] Sidónio's speech from the balcony of the Grand Hotel, Porto, 12 January 1918.

[32] Serrão (1989: 199-200) does point out that Sidónio's statements to the army, particularly those made in respect of Portugal's involvement in the war and which were the only statements he made that offered a tangible promise they knew regime would honour all its war commitments. The reason Sidónio was at pains to make his position on this subject clear was the need to quell rumours that he was pro-German.

[33] The Constitutionalists were those monarchists who supported Manuel II, the king who had been deposed by the 5 October 1910 revolution, and who sought the restoration of the constitutional monarchy as it existed prior to the Republic.

[34] Martino Nobre de Melo was appointed Justice Minister on 8 March 1918. He had been a colleague of Raposo during their time at Coimbra University where they both studied law. Earning their living in Lisbon, Nobre de Melo and Raposo lived close to each other and often dined together.

[35] Braga da Cruz (1980: 21) enumerates the alterations made by Sidónio's regime to the Law of Separation: the need for a licence to hold mass at certain times was abolished; state supervision of seminaries was ended; the *beneplácito* was abolished (the need for the church to obtain state permission to publish documents or appoint priests), as well the state pensions conceded to the *widows* and children of priests; the right to wear clerical vestments was restored. A law of February 1918 also restored ownership of Church buildings and all objects essential for divine worship to the parishes.

[36] Compare this appeal with Sidónio's statement of 15 January: 'I will accept all honest and well-intentioned men without regard to their political or religious beliefs'.

[37] As diplomatic relations with the Portuguese state had been severed by the Vatican on 24 May 1911 (with the publication of the encyclical *Iamdudum in Portugal*) because of the Law of Separation, the withdrawal of this legislation was a prerequisite for these relations to be restored.

[38] The 1911 constitution contained several articles that were not acceptable to the Catholic Church, especially Article 3.8: 'The public profession of any religion may be conducted in the houses chosen or destined for that purpose by the followers of that religion... However, in the inter-

ests of public order and to ensure the freedom and security of all citizens, a special law will determine the conditions of this right'; Article 3.9: 'Public cemeteries will be secular, in which all religious services and rights may be practised to the extent that they do not offend public morality, the principles of public right and the law'; Article 3.10: 'Education administered in public and private establishments that are supervised by the state shall be the non-religious'; and Article 3.12: 'The legislation disbanding the Company of Jesus and its affiliates in Portugal, whatever their denomination, and expelling all religious congregations and monastic quarters and prohibiting their return to Portuguese territory, is hereby maintained'. Assembleia da República (1992: 196).

[39] This decision was made public by Sidónio in a speech in Évora on 15 February 1918: 'It is necessary to form a party comprising everyone and to realise the work of the Republic'.

[40] These proposals were made public by Sidónio during a speech in Beja on 17 February 1918: 'An absolutist regime is not possible in the 20th century, which means we must opt for a republican regime. However, for this we need the country to pronounce upon the type of regime we must choose—whether parliamentary or presidentialist. The former has already failed; the latter is the new idea!'

[41] For example, see Gregor (1979: 135) who believes that a strong regime party is necessary for the creation and maintenance of a 'strong state capable of articulating a national policy that would co-ordinate all the parochial, regional and special interests of the nation in a collective undertaking calculated to foster economic expansion and rationalisation'.

[42] Unlike in Italy during the period 1919-21, when the groups that coalesced into the fascist movement were developing detailed economic and political programmes for the future fascist state, Sidónio's supporters during the period 1916-18 were too busy concentrating on short-term political expedients designed primarily to remove the Democrats. The only political movement in Portugal at that time that had developed its own doctrine, and which was capable of supplying Sidonismo with a political and economic programme was the Integralists. However, as we have seen, their monarchism was an effective bar to their full inclusion, as that would have alienated the Republican and urban sectors the new regime also hoped to incorporate.

[43] Schaar (1981: 20-5) argues legitimacy is not necessarily a product of a regime's origins, but more often it is the result of its ability to achieve

its goals—that is, it is a consequence of its ability to generate desires and then to manage and ultimately satisfy these passions. Sidonismo was able to provide a focus for groups opposed to the Democratic Party in the immediate wake of his coup; however, it was unable to provide solutions that would satisfy sufficient numbers of these groups without generating substantial opposition within the coalition. Acquiescence to the regime, built upon the stated aims of restoring order and ending the Democratic demagogy, was sufficient to ensure the regime's short-term security, however, having restored order and ended the Democrats' rule, the regime was left grappling with the political question, a fact noted by the leaders of Integralism (see Raposo 1945).

[44] For more on the background to the Catholic church's decision to contest the elections separately, see Braga da Cruz (1980: 270-4). For a discussion of the Integralists decision to include themselves in the separate monarchist list, see Raposo (1945: 35-40). Ribeiro de Meneses (1998b) suggests Brito Camacho's decision to withdraw his support from the regime was based on his discomfiture at the Bonapartist 'personality cult' that was being developed around Sidónio, believing the PNR was intended to be little more than a vehicle for this cult.

[45] The case of Italian Fascism is instructive here. Mussolini came to power in 1922 with the support of several disparate groups, ranging from the distributionist 'social' fascists led by Rossoni, through the productionist nationalists whose intellectual leader was Alberto Rocco, and the black shirted *Squadristi* led by Italo Balbo. Mussolini's regime did not begin to adopt a coherent programme until after his acceptance of responsibility for the assassination of the socialist leader Giacomo Matteoti in 1925.

[46] Weber identified three sources of political legitimacy: legal, traditional and charismatic. In a revolutionary situation in which a small group succeeds in overthrowing a legally established regime, either with or without the support of large sections of society, the revolutionaries must seek to legitimise their rule by appeal to at least one of these three sources of legitimacy. Sidónio was no exception to this and made his initial appeals based on legality and tradition. His argument that his regime was legitimate was the most pronounced aspect of his early statements that he was acting to end the Democratic demagogy and is implicit in his statement of 13 January 1918 that 'revolutions are made by a minority who are almost always opposed by the majority. However, despite this, no revolution is possible unless the people are with it spiritually'. The appeal to traditional legitimacy was a constant in the Sidonista regime's public pronouncements prior to the

presidential election of May 1918. For example, on 12 December 1917, Sidónio said that: 'We will dedicate ourselves to regenerating our customs and reintegrate the Republic and strengthen the motherland', and on 4 March 1918: 'We want a Portugal that is in tune with its history and its traditions, that can live honourably among the civilised nations with which it is linked'.

[47] Situationism describes a process through which political elites are accommodated into a new political system. Robinson (1979: 33) equates it with political opportunism, through which individuals accommodate themselves to the new system to ensure their survival and or advancement. The inclusion of political elites is normally achieved, at least in the Portuguese case, by a system of rewards and threats.

[48] Sidónio's speech following his election as President, 9 May 1918.

[49] Sidónio's speech at Santarém, 4 March 1918.

[50] Sidónio's speech at Santarém, 4 March 1918.

[51] That is, its subjective propagandistic role as a mass-mobilisation body and its objective role as a demobilisation and sterilising body.

[52] External in the sense that it was advanced by the party and not by the regime.

[53] The lack of a constitutional settlement did cause problems for Sidónio in the medium-term as it prevented the formal closure of the regime question.

[54] There is a profusion of evidence from Sidónio's own public statements in support of this assertion, much of which has been presented above.

[55] This is precisely what did happen with the Monarchy of the North and the Monsanto Uprising in January 1919, one month after Sidónio's death.

References

Arquivo Histórico Militar, 1 Div 35 Sec Cx 1279, *Depoimento de Machado Santos Sobre o 13 de Dezembro de 1916.*

— 1 Div 35 Sec Cx 1279, *Relatório Sobre os Tumultos em Penafiel, 8 Julho 1917.*

Constituições Portuguesas (1992), Lisbon: Assembleia da República.

Barreira, C. (1982a), 'Homem Cristo Filho: Algumas considerações em torno do seu percurso'. *Fascismo em Portugal: Actas de um Colóquio, Março 1980,* Lisbon: A Regra do Jogo.

— (1982b), 'Três nótulas sobre o Integralismo Lusitano (evolução, descontinuidade, ideologia nas páginas da Nação Portuguesa, 1914-26), *Análise Social* XVIII (3-5), pp. 1421-9.

Bourne, K. and Watt, D. C. (eds) (1993), *British Documents on Foreign Affairs: Reports and Papers from the Foreign Office Confidential Print. Part II. From the First to the Second World War. Series F. Europe 1919-39—Portugal,* Washington DC: University Publications of America.

Braga da Cruz, M. (1980a), *As Origens da Democracia Cristã e o Salazarismo,* Lisbon: Presença.

— (1982), 'O Integralismo Lusitano e o Estado Novo', *Fascismo em Portugal: Actas de um Colóquio, Março 1980,* Lisbon: A Regra do Jogo.

— (1986), *Monarquicos e Republicanos no Estado Novo,* Lisbon: Dom Quixote.

— (1995), 'Salazarismo e o fascismo', paper presented to the Fundación Pablo Iglesias conference, *Los Riesgos de la Democracia: Fascismo y Neofascismo,* Madrid, 16-17 November.

Brito, A. J. de (1996), *Para a Compreensão do Pensamento*

Contra-Revolucionário, Alfredo Pimenta, António Sardinha, Charles Maurras, Salazar, Lisbon: Hugin.

Cardoso, M. E. (1982), 'Misticismo e ideologia no contexto cultural português: A saudade, o sebastianismo e o Integralismo Lusitano', *Análise Social* XVIII (3-5), pp. 1399-1408.

Costa Pinto, A. (1982), 'A formação do Integralismo Lusitano', *Análise Social* XVIII (3-5), pp. 1409-19.

Diuturnum (1891), Encyclical of Pope Leo XIII, 29 June.

Farelo Lopes, F. (1992), *Poder Político e Caciquismo na Primeira República Portuguesa,* Lisbon: Estampa.

Ferreira, J. M. (1992), *O Comportamento Político dos Militares: Forças Armadas e Regimes Políticos em Portugal no Século XX,* Lisbon: Estampa.

Figueiredo, A. de (1975), *Portugal: Fifty Years of Dictatorship,* Harmondsworth: Penguin.

Georgel, J. (1985), *O Salazarismo,* Lisbon: Dom Quixote.

Iamdudum (1911), Encyclical of Pope Pius X, 24 May,

Imortale Dei (1885), Encyclical of Pope Leo XIII, 1 November.

Levy, K. (1999), 'Fascism, National Socialism and conservatives in Europe, 1914-45: Issues for comparison', *Contemporary European History* 6 (1), pp.97-126.

Libertas (1888), Encyclical of Pope Leo XIII, 20 June.

Lloyd-Jones, J. S. (1999), 'Action Française and Integralismo Lusitano: A critical comparison', *University of Dundee Department of Politics Occasional Papers.*

Lucena, M. de (1979), 'The evolution of Portuguese corporatism under Salazar and Caetano', in L. S. Graham and H. M. Makler (eds), *Contemporary Portugal: The Revolution and its Antecedents,* Austin, TX: University of Texas Press.

Medina, J. (1978), *Salazar e os Fascistas: Salazarismo*

e Nacional Sindicalismo. A História de um Conflito, 1932-45, Lisbon: Bertrand.

Meneses, F. R. de (1998a), 'Too serious a matter to be left to the generals? Parliament and the army in wartime Portugal', *Journal of Contemporary History* 33 (1), pp. 85-96.

— (1998b), 'Sidónio Pais, the Portuguese New Republic and the challenge to liberalism in Southern Europe', *European History Quarterly* 28 (1), pp. 109-30.

Nogueira, F. (1977), *Salazar*, Vol. I. *A Mocidade e os Princípios*, Coimbra: Atlântida.

Oliveira Marques, A. H. de (1972), *History of Portugal*. Vol. II. *From Empire to Corporate State*, New York, NY: Columbia University Press.

— (1975), *A Primeira República Portuguesa: Alguns Aspectos Estruturais*, Lisbon: Horizonte.

Pais, J. M. (1988), 'A crise do regime liberal republicano: Algumas hipóteses explicativas', *O Estado Novo*, Vol. I. *Das Origens ao fim da Autarquia, 1926-59*, Lisbon: Fragmentos.

Proença, R. (1921a), 'Acerca do Integralismo Lusitano', *Seara Nova*, 24 December.

— (1921b), 'O que é o Integralismo', *Seara Nova*, 24 December.

— (1922a), 'As contradicções íntimas do nacionalismo integralista', *Seara Nova*, 14 January.

— (1922b), 'Política das ideias e política do facto', *Seara Nova*, 1 February.

— (1922c), 'Liberdade e igualdade', *Seara Nova*, 1 March.

— (1922d), 'O progresso e as doutrinas científicas', *Seara Nova*, 1 April.

— (1922e), 'Nacionalismo e internacionalism', *Seara Nova*, 1 July.

Ecos do Minho (1917),'Programa do Centro Católica', 22 August.

Raposo, H. (1945), *Folhas do meu Cadastro.* Vol. I. *1911-23,* Lisbon: Gama.

Os Ridículos (1916-18).

Rol de Deshonra (1917), 5 September.

Salazar, O. de A. (1917), 'Alguns aspectos da crise das subsistências', *Boletim da Faculdade de Direito de Coimbra,* IV.

Sardinha, A. (1915), *O Valor da Raça: Introdução a uma Campanha Nacional,* Lisbon: Almeida, Miranda e Sousa.

— (1916), *A Questão Ibérica: Antecedentes e Possibilidades,* Lisbon: Almeida, Miranda e Sousa.

— (1924), *Ao Princípio ero o Verbo: Ensaios e Estudos,* Lisbon: Portugália.

— (1925), *Ao Ritmo da Ampulheta: Crítica e História,* Lisbon: Lumen.

— (1929), *Purgartório das Ideias; Ensaios e Crítica,* Lisbon: Ferin.

— (1934), *A Prol do Comum: Doutrinas e História,* Lisbon: Ferin.

— (1937), *Processo dum Rei,* Porto: Civilização.

O Século Cómico (1916-18).

Serrão, J. V. (1989), *História de Portugal.* Vol. XI. *A Primeira República (1912-26): História, Política, Religiosa, Militar e Ultramarina,* Lisbon: Verbo.

Schwartzmann, K. (1988a), 'Instabilidade democrática nos países semiperiférica: A Primeira República Portuguesa', *O Estado Novo.* Vol. I. *Das Origens ao fim da Autarquia, 1926-59,* Lisbon: Fragmentos.

— (1988b), *The Social Origins of Democratic Collapse: The*

First Portuguese Republic in the Global Economy, Lawrence, KS: University of Kansas Press.

Wheeler, D. L. (1972), 'The Portuguese Revolution of 1910', *Journal of Modern History* 44 (2), pp. 172-94.

Thank you

Thank you once again for purchasing this book! We sincerely hope you found it useful and interesting.

Now that you have finished it, we would be incredibly grateful if you could take a moment to leave an honest review on Amazon. Your feedback is essential to us and helps others make informed decisions about their reading choices.

Honest reviews, whether positive or constructive, play a crucial role in supporting our small business and enabling us to improve.

Thank you once again for your purchase and for being part of our journey. We look forward to hearing your thoughts on our book!

To leave a review, please follow these steps:
1. Go to Amazon and search for the product name or ASIN.
2. Navigate to the product page.
3. Scroll down to the reviews section.
4. Click on "Write a customer review" to leave your feedback.

www.ingramcontent.com/pod-product-compliance
Lightning Source LLC
La Vergne TN
LVHW050333160826
845677LV00014B/3610

* 9 7 9 8 2 2 7 9 8 2 7 9 7 *